HIGH
AND LOW

BY
JOHN BETJEMAN

LONDON
JOHN MURRAY, ALBEMARLE STREET

By the same author

Poems

A FEW LATE CHRYSANTHEMUMS

COLLECTED POEMS

SUMMONED BY BELLS

A RING OF BELLS

Prose

FIRST AND LAST LOVES

First Edition November 1966
Reprinted November 1966
Reprinted January 1967

© John Betjeman 1959, 1960, 1961,
1962, 1963, 1964, 1965, 1966

Printed in Great Britain by
William Clowes and Sons, Limited
London and Beccles

HIGH AND LOW

Contents

CONTENTS

LIGHT AND DARK

PERSONAL

To

Candida and Rupert

MURRAY, you bid my plastic pen
A preface write. Well, here's one then.
Verse seems to me the shortest way
Of saying what one has to say,
A memorable means of dealing
With mood or person, place or feeling.
Anything extra that is given
Is taken as a gift from Heaven.

 The English language has such range,
Such rhymes and half-rhymes, rhythms strange,
And such variety of tone,
It is a music of its own.
With MILTON *it has organ power*
As loud as bells in Redcliffe tower;
It falls like winter crisp and light
On COWPER's *Buckinghamshire night,*
It can be gentle as a lake,
Where WORDSWORTH's *oars a ripple make*
Or rest with TENNYSON *at ease*
In sibilance of summer seas,
Or languorous as lilies grow,
When DOWSON's *lamp is burning low –*
For endless changes can be rung
On church-bells of the English tongue.

 MURRAY, your venerable door
Opened to BYRON, CRABBE *and* MOORE
And TOMMY CAMPBELL. *How can I,*
A buzzing insubstantial fly,
Compare with them? I do not try,
Pleased simply to be one who shares
An imprint that was also theirs,
And grateful to the people who
Have bought my verses hitherto.

Acknowledgements

The author is grateful to his friends Lord
Birkenhead and Thomas Edward Neil Driberg.
The first decided which poems were to be pub-
lished, and the second corrected grammar and
punctuation, and changed some lines for the
better.   He thanks the editors of *The Atlantic
Monthly, The Cornhill, Encounter, London
Magazine, The New Yorker, The Observer,
Vogue, Weekend Telegraph, The Philbeach
Quarterly* and *Punch* for permission to reprint
some of the verses in this book.   The Harvest
Hymn was published as a letter in *The Farmers
Weekly.*

LANDSCAPES

Cornish Cliffs

Those moments, tasted once and never done,
Of long surf breaking in the mid-day sun,
A far-off blow-hole booming like a gun—

The seagulls plane and circle out of sight
Below this thirsty, thrift-encrusted height,
The veined sea-campion buds burst into white

And gorse turns tawny orange, seen beside
Pale drifts of primroses cascading wide
To where the slate falls sheer into the tide.

More than in gardened Surrey, nature spills
A wealth of heather, kidney-vetch and squills
Over these long-defended Cornish hills.

A gun-emplacement of the latest war
Looks older than the hill fort built before
Saxon or Norman headed for the shore.

3

And in the shadowless, unclouded glare
Deep blue above us fades to whiteness where
A misty sea-line meets the wash of air.

Nut-smell of gorse and honey-smell of ling
Waft out to sea the freshness of the spring
On sunny shallows, green and whispering.

The wideness which the lark-song gives the sky
Shrinks at the clang of sea-birds sailing by
Whose notes are tuned to days when seas are high.

From today's calm, the lane's enclosing green
Leads inland to a usual Cornish scene—
Slate cottages with sycamore between,

Small fields and tellymasts and wires and poles
With, as the everlasting ocean rolls,
Two chapels built for half a hundred souls

Tregardock

A mist that from the moor arose
    In sea-fog wraps Port Isaac bay,
The moan of warning from Trevose
    Makes grimmer this October day.

Only the shore and cliffs are clear.
    Gigantic slithering shelves of slate
In waiting awfulness appear
    Like journalism full of hate.

On the steep path a bramble leaf
    Stands motionless and wet with dew,
The grass bends down, the bracken's brown,
    The grey-green gorse alone is new.

Cautious my sliding footsteps go
    To quarried rock and dripping cave;
The ocean, leaden-still below,
    Hardly has strength to lift a wave.

I watch it crisp into its height
    And flap exhausted on the beach,
The long surf menacing and white
    Hissing as far as it can reach.

The dunlin do not move, each bird
    Is stationary on the sand
As if a spirit in it heard
    The final end of sea and land.

And I on my volcano edge
    Exposed to ridicule and hate
Still do not dare to leap the ledge
    And smash to pieces on the slate.

By the Ninth Green, St Enodoc

Dark of primaeval pine encircles me
With distant thunder of an angry sea
While wrack and resin scent alternately
    The air I breathe.

On slate compounded before man was made
The ocean ramparts roll their light and shade
Up to Bray Hill and, leaping to invade,
    Fall back and seethe.

A million years of unrelenting tide
Have smoothed the strata of the steep cliffside:
How long ago did rock with rock collide
    To shape these hills?

One day the mayfly's life, three weeks the cleg's,
The woodworm's four-year cycle bursts its eggs,
The flattened centipede lets loose its legs
    And stings and kills.

Hot life pulsating in this foreshore dry,
Damp life upshooting from the reed-beds high,
Under those barrows, dark against the sky,
    The Iron Age dead—

Why is it that a sunlit second sticks?
What force collects all this and seeks to fix
This fourth March morning nineteen sixty-six
    Deep in my head?

Winter Seascape

The sea runs back against itself
  With scarcely time for breaking wave
To cannonade a slatey shelf
  And thunder under in a cave

Before the next can fully burst.
  The headwind, blowing harder still,
Smooths it to what it was at first—
  A slowly rolling water-hill.

Against the breeze the breakers haste,
  Against the tide their ridges run
And all the sea's a dappled waste
  Criss-crossing underneath the sun.

Far down the beach the ripples drag
  Blown backward, rearing from the shore,
And wailing gull and shrieking shag
  Alone can pierce the ocean roar.

Unheard, a mongrel hound gives tongue,
　　Unheard are shouts of little boys:
What chance has any inland lung
　　Against this multi-water noise?

Here where the cliffs alone prevail
　　I stand exultant, neutral, free,
And from the cushion of the gale
　　Behold a huge consoling sea.

Old Friends

The sky widens to Cornwall.   A sense of sea
  Hangs in the lichenous branches and still there's light.
The road from its tunnel of blackthorn rises free
      To a final height,

And over the west is glowing a mackerel sky
  Whose opal fleece has faded to purple pink.
In this hour of the late-lit, listening evening, why
      Do my spirits sink?

The tide is high and a sleepy Atlantic sends
  Exploring ripple on ripple down Polzeath shore,
And the gathering dark is full of the thought of friends
      I shall see no more.

Where is Anne Channel who loved this place the best,
  With her tense blue eyes and her shopping-bag falling
                                        apart,
And her racy gossip and nineteen-twenty zest,
      And that warmth of heart?

11

Where's Roland, easing his most unwieldy car

   With its load of golf-clubs, backwards into the lane?

Where Kathleen Stokes with her Sealyhams? There's
                                 Doom Bar;
      Bray Hill shows plain:

For this is the turn, and the well-known trees draw near;

   On the road their pattern in moonlight fades and swells:

As the engine stops, from two miles off I hear

      St Minver bells.

What a host of stars in a wideness still and deep:

   What a host of souls, as a motor-bike whines away

And the silver snake of the estuary curls to sleep

      In Daymer Bay.

Are they one with the Celtic saints and the years between?

   Can they see the moonlit pools where ribbonweed drifts?

As I reach our hill, I am part of a sea unseen—

      The oppression lifts.

A Bay in Anglesey

The sleepy sound of a tea-time tide
Slaps at the rocks the sun has dried,

Too lazy, almost, to sink and lift
Round low peninsulas pink with thrift.

The water, enlarging shells and sand,
Grows greener emerald out from land

And brown over shadowy shelves below
The waving forests of seaweed show.

Here at my feet in the short cliff grass
Are shells, dried bladderwrack, broken glass,

Pale blue squills and yellow rock roses.
The next low ridge that we climb discloses

One more field for the sheep to graze
While, scarcely seen on this hottest of days,

Far to the eastward, over there,
Snowdon rises in pearl-grey air.

Multiple lark-song, whispering bents,
The thymy, turfy and salty scents

And filling in, brimming in, sparkling and free
The sweet susurration of incoming sea.

A Lament for Moira McCavendish

Through the midlands of Ireland I journeyed by diesel
    And bright in the sun shone the emerald plain;
Though loud sang the birds on the thorn-bush and teasel
    They could not be heard for the sound of the train.

The roll of the railway made musing creative:
    I thought of the colleen I soon was to see
With her wiry black hair and grey eyes of the native,
    Sweet Moira McCavendish, acushla machree.

Her brother's wee cabin stands distant from Tallow
    A league and a half, where the Blackwater flows,
And the musk and potato, the mint and the mallow
    Do grow there in beauty, along with the rose.

'Twas smoothly we raced through the open expansion
    Of rush-covered levels and gate-lodge and gate
And the ruined demesne and the windowless mansion
    Where once the oppressor had revelled in state.

15

At Castletownroche, as the prospect grew hillier,
  I saw the far mountains to Moira long-known
Till I came to the valley and townland familiar
  With the Protestant church standing locked and alone.

O vein of my heart! upon Tallow Road Station
  No face was to greet me, so freckled and white;
As the diesel slid out, leaving still desolation,
  The McCavendish ass-cart was nowhere in sight.

For a league and half to the Blackwater river
  I tramped with my bundle her cabin to see
And herself by the fuchsias, her young lips a-quiver
  Half-smiling, half-weeping a welcome to me.

Och Moira McCavendish! the fangs of the creeper
  Have struck at the thatch and thrust open the door;
The couch in the garden grows ranker and deeper
  Than musk and potato which bloomed there before.

Flow on, you remorseless and salmon-full waters!
  What care I for prospects so silvery fair?
The heart in me's dead, like your sweetest of daughters,
  And I would that my spirit were lost on the air.

The Small Towns of Ireland

Public houses in Irish country towns are very often
general merchants as well. You drink at a counter
with bacon on it. Brooms and plastic dustpans hang
from the ceiling. Loaves of new bread are stacked
on top of fuse wire and, over all, there is a deep,
delicious silence that can be found only in Ireland,
in the midlands of Ireland in particular—the least
touristed and profoundest part of that whole sad,
beautiful country. Much that is native and tradi-
tional goes on, including the printing of ballads in
metres derived from the Celts via Tom Moore.
These ballads are called hedge poetry and their
authors are the last descendants of the Gaelic bards.
It was in just such a general shop as I have described
that I might have found, pinned up among the no-
tices for a local Feis, Gaelic football matches and
Government proclamations, the following ballad,
printed on emerald paper in a border of shamrocks.

The small towns of Ireland by bards are neglected,

They stand there, all lonesome, on hilltop and plain.

The Protestant glebe house by beech trees protected

Sits close to the gates of his Lordship's demesne.

But where is his Lordship, who once in a phaeton

Drove out twixt his lodges and into the town?

Oh his tragic misfortunes I will not dilate on;
　　His mansion's a ruin, his woods are cut down.

His impoverished descendant is dwelling in Ealing,
　　His daughters must type for their bread and their board,
O'er the graves of his forebears the nettle is stealing
　　And few will remember the sad Irish Lord.

Yet still stands the Mall where his agent resided,
　　The doctor, attorney and such class of men.
The elegant fanlights and windows provided
　　A Dublin-like look for the town's Upper Ten.

'Twas bravely they stood by the Protestant steeple
　　As over the town rose their roof-trees afar.
Let us slowly descend to the part where the people
　　Do mingle their ass-carts by Finnegan's bar.

I hear it once more, the soft sound of those voices,
　　When fair day is filling with farmers the Square,
And the heart in my bosom delights and rejoices
　　To think of the dealing and drinking done there.

I see thy grey granite, O grim House of Sessions !
　　I think of the judges who sat there in state

And my mind travels back to our monster processions
    To honour the heroes of brave Ninety-Eight.

The barracks are burned where the Redcoats oppressed us,
    The gaol is broke open, our people are free.
Though Cromwell once cursed us, Saint Patrick has blessed
                                                    us —
    The merciless English have fled o'er the sea.

Look out where yon cabins grow smaller to smallest,
    Straw-thatched and one-storey and soon to come down,
To the prominent steeple, the newest and tallest
    Of Saint Malachy's Catholic Church in our town:

The fine architécture, the wealth of mosaic,
    The various marbles on altars within—
To attempt a description were merely prosaic,
    So, asking your pardon, I will not begin.

O my small town of Ireland, the raindrops caress you,
    The sun sparkles bright on your field and your Square
As here on your bridge I salute you and bless you,
    Your murmuring waters and turf-scented air.

Ireland's Own
or
The Burial of Thomas Moore

In the churchyard of Bromham the yews intertwine
O'er a smooth granite cross of a Celtic design,
Looking quite out of place in surroundings like these
In a corner of Wilts 'twixt the chalk and the cheese.

I can but account you neglected and poor,
Dear bard of my boyhood, mellifluous Moore,
That far from the land which of all you loved best
In a village of England your bones should have rest.

I had rather they lay where the Blackwater glides
When the light of the evening doth burnish its tides
And St Carthage Cathedral's meticulous spire
Is tipped like the Castle with sun-setting fire.

I had rather some gate-lodge of plaster and thatch
With slim pointed windows and porches to match

Had last seen your coffin drawn out on the road
From a great Irish house to its final abode.

Or maybe a rath with a round tower near
And the whispering Shannon delighting the ear
And the bog all around and the width of the sky
Is the place where your bones should deservedly lie.

The critics may scorn you and Hazlitt may carp
At the ' Musical Snuff-box ' you made of the Harp;
The Regency drawing-rooms that thrilled with your song
Are not the true world to which now you belong.

No! the lough and the mountain, the ruins and rain
And purple-blue distances bound your demesne,
For the tunes to the elegant measures you trod
Have chords of deep longing for Ireland and God.

Great Central Railway
Sheffield Victoria to Banbury

' Unmitigated England '
   Came swinging down the line
That day the February sun
   Did crisp and crystal shine.
Dark red at Kirkby Bentinck stood
   A steeply gabled farm
Mid ash trees and a sycamore
   In charismatic calm.
A village street—a manor house—
   A church—then, tally ho!
We pounded through a housing scheme
   With tellymasts a-row,
Where cars of parked executives
   Did regimented wait
Beside administrative blocks
   Within the factory gate.
She waved to us from Hucknall South
   As we hooted round a bend

22

From a curtained front-room window did
    The diesel driver's friend.
Through cuttings deep to Nottingham
    Precariously we wound;
The swallowing tunnel made the train
    Seem London's Underground.
Above the fields of Leicestershire
    On arches we were borne
And the rumble of the railway drowned
    The thunder of the Quorn;
And silver shone the steeples out
    Above the barren boughs;
Colts in a paddock ran from us
    But not the solid cows;
And quite where Rugby Central is
    Does only Rugby know.
We watched the empty platform wait
    And sadly saw it go.
By now the sun of afternoon
    Showed ridge and furrow shadows
And shallow unfamiliar lakes
    Stood shivering in the meadows.
Is Woodford church or Hinton church
    The one I ought to see?

Or were they both too much restored
    In 1883 ?
I do not know.   Towards the west
    A trail of glory runs
And we leave the old Great Central line
    For Banbury and buns.

Matlock Bath

From Matlock Bath's half-timbered station
    I see the black dissenting spire—
Thin witness of a congregation,
    Stone emblem of a Handel choir;
In blest Bethesda's limpid pool
Comes treacling out of Sunday School.

By cool Siloam's shady rill—
    The sounds are sweet as strawberry jam:
I raise mine eyes unto the hill,
    The beetling HEIGHTS OF ABRAHAM;
The branchy trees are white with rime
In Matlock Bath this winter-time,

And from the whiteness, grey uprearing,
    Huge cliffs hang sunless ere they fall,
A tossed and stony ocean nearing
    The moment to o'erwhelm us all:

25

Eternal Father, strong to save,
How long wilt thou suspend the wave?

How long before the pleasant acres
    Of intersecting LOVERS' WALKS
Are rolled across by limestone breakers,
    Whole woodlands snapp'd like cabbage stalks?
O God, our help in ages past,
How long will SPEEDWELL CAVERN last?

In this dark dale I hear the thunder
    Of houses folding with the shocks,
The GRAND PAVILION buckling under
    The weight of the ROMANTIC ROCKS,
The hardest Blue John ash-trays seem
To melt away in thermal steam.

Deep in their Nonconformist setting
    The shivering children wait their doom—
The father's whip, the mother's petting
    In many a coffee-coloured room;
And attic bedrooms shriek with fright,
For dread of *Pilgrims of the Night.*

Perhaps it's this that makes me shiver

    As I ascend the slippery path

High, high above the sliding river

    And terraces of Matlock Bath:

A sense of doom, a dread to see

The *Rock of Ages cleft for me.*

An Edwardian Sunday
Broomhill, Sheffield

High dormers are rising
So sharp and surprising,
And ponticum edges
The driveways of gravel;
Stone houses from ledges
Look down on ravines.
The vision can travel
From gable to gable,
Italianate mansion
And turretted stable,
A sylvan expansion
So varied and jolly
Where laurel and holly
Commingle their greens.

Serene on a Sunday
The sun glitters hotly
O'er mills that on Monday

With engines will hum.
By tramway excursion
To Dore and to Totley
In search of diversion
The millworkers come;
But in our arboreta
The sounds are discreeter
Of shoes upon stone —
The worshippers wending
To welcoming chapel,
Companioned or lone;
And over a pew there
See loveliness lean,
As Eve shows her apple
Through rich bombazine:
What love is born new there
In blushing eighteen!

Your prospects will please her,
The iron-king's daughter,
Up here on Broomhill:
Strange Hallamshire, County
Of dearth and of bounty,
Of brown tumbling water
And furnace and mill.

Your own Ebenezer*

Looks down from his height

On back street and alley

And chemical valley

Laid out in the light;

On ugly and pretty

Where industry thrives

In this hill-shadowed city

Of razors and knives.

* The statue of Ebenezer Elliott (1781–1849) the 'Corn Law Rhymer' outside the Mappin Gallery, Sheffield.

Lines written to Martyn Skinner before his departure from Oxfordshire in search of quiet—1961

Return, return to Ealing,
　Worn poet of the farm!
Regain your boyhood feeling
　Of uninvaded calm!
For there the leafy avenues
　Of lime and chestnut mix'd
Do widely wind, by art designed,
　The costly houses 'twixt.

No early morning tractors
　The thrush and blackbird drown,
No nuclear reactors
　Bulge hideous on the down,
No youth upon his motor-bike
　His lust for power fulfils
With dentist's drill intent to kill
　The silence of the hills.

In Ealing on a Sunday
   Bell-haunted quiet falls,
In Ealing on a Monday
   'Milk-o!' the milkman calls;
No lorries grind in bottom gear
   Up steep and narrow lanes,
Nor constant here offend the ear
   Low-flying aeroplanes.

Return, return to Ealing,
   Worn poet of the farm!
Regain your boyhood feeling
   Of uninvaded calm!
Where smoothly glides the bicycle
   And softly flows the Brent
And a gentle gale from Perivale
   Sends up the hayfield scent.

Uffington

Tonight we feel the muffled peal
   Hang on the village like a pall;
It overwhelms the towering elms—
   That death-reminding dying fall;
The very sky no longer high
   Comes down within the reach of all.
Imprisoned in a cage of sound
Even the trivial seems profound.

PORTRAITS

Anglo-Catholic Congresses

We, who remember the Faith, the grey-headed ones,
   Of those Anglo-Catholic Congresses swinging along,
Who heard the South Coast salvo of incense-guns
   And surged to the Albert Hall in our thousands strong
   With 'extreme' colonial bishops leading in song;

We, who remember, look back to the blossoming May-time
   On ghosts of servers and thurifers after Mass,
The slapping of backs, the flapping of cassocks, the play-
                       time,
   A game of Grandmother's Steps on the vicarage grass—
   "Father, a little more sherry.　I'll fill your glass."

We recall the triumph, that Sunday after Ascension,
   When our Protestant suffragan suffered himself to be
                       coped—
The SYA and the Scheme for Church Extension —
   The new diocesan's not as 'sound' as we'd hoped,
   And Kensit threatens and has Sam Gurney poped?

Yet, under the Travers baroque, in a limewashed whiteness,
  The fiddle-back vestments a-glitter with morning rays,
Our Lady's image, in multiple-candled brightness,
  The bells and banners—those were the waking days
  When Faith was taught and fanned to a golden blaze.

In Willesden Churchyard

Come walk with me, my love, to Neasden Lane.
The chemicals from various factories
Have bitten deep into the Portland stone
And streaked the white Carrara of the graves
Of many a Pooter and his Caroline,
Long laid to rest among these dripping trees;
And that small heap of fast-decaying flowers
Marks Lupin Pooter lately gathered in;
And this, my love, is Laura Seymour's grave—
' So long the loyal counsellor and friend '
Of that Charles Reade whose coffin lies with hers.
Was she his mistress?   Did he visit her
When coming down from Oxford by the coach?
Alighting at the turnpike, did he walk
These elmy lanes of Middlesex and climb
A stile or two across the dairy farms
Over to Harlesden at the wicket gate?
Then the soft rigours of his Fellowship
Were tenderly relaxed.   The sun would send

Last golden streaks of mild October light
On tarred and weather-boarded barn and shed.
Blue bonfire smoke would hang among the trees;
And in the little stucco hermitage
Did Laura gently stroke her lover's head?
And did her Charles look up into her eyes
For loyal counsel there?   I do not know.
Doubtless some pedant for his Ph.D.
Has ascertained the facts, or I myself
Might find them in the public libraries.
I only know that as we see her grave
My flesh, to dissolution nearer now
Than yours, which is so milky white and soft,
Frightens me, though the Blessed Sacrament
Not ten yards off in Willesden parish church
Glows with the present immanence of God.

The Commander

On a shining day of October we remembered you,
                                                Commander,
  When the trees were gold and still

And some of their boughs were green where the whip of the
                                        wind had missed them
  On this nippy Staffordshire hill.

A clean sky streamed through institutional windows

  As we heard the whirr of Time

Touching our Quaker silence, in builders' lorries departing

  For Newcastle-under-Lyme.

The proving words of the psalm you bequeathed to the
                                                gowned assembly
  On waiting silence broke,

' Lord, I am not high-minded . . .'   In the youthful voice
                                                of the student
  Your own humility spoke.

I remembered our shared delight in architecture and nature

  As bicycling we went

By saffron-spotted palings to crumbling box-pewed churches

Down hazel lanes in Kent.

I remembered on winter evenings, with wine and the family
round you,

Your reading Dickens aloud

And the laughs we used to have at your gift for administra-
tion,

For you were never proud.

Sky and sun and the sea! the greatness of things was in you

And thus you refrained your soul.

Let others fuss over academical detail,

You saw people whole.

' Lord, I am not high-minded . . . '   The final lesson you
taught me,

When you bade the world good-bye,

Was humbly and calmly to trust in the soul's survival

When my own hour comes to die.

Autumn 1964

(FOR KAREN)

Red apples hang like globes of light
  Against this pale November haze,
And now, although the mist is white,
  In half-an-hour a day of days
Will climb into its golden height
  And Sunday bells will ring its praise.

The sparkling flint, the darkling yew,
  The red brick, less intensely red
Than hawthorn berries bright with dew
  Or leaves of creeper still unshed,
The watery sky washed clean and new,
  Are all rejoicing with the dead.

The yellowing elm shows yet some green,
  The mellowing bells exultant sound:
Never have light and colour been
  So prodigally thrown around;
And, in the bells, the promise tells
  Of greater light where Love is found.

43

The Hon. Sec.

The flag that hung half-mast to-day
   Seemed animate with being
As if it knew for whom it flew
   And will no more be seeing.

He loved each corner of the links—
   The stream at the eleventh,
The grey-green bents, the pale sea-pinks,
   The prospect from the seventh;

To the ninth tee the uphill climb,
   A grass and sandy stairway,
And at the top the scent of thyme
   And long extent of fairway.

He knew how on a summer day
   The sea's deep blue grew deeper,
How evening shadows over Bray
   Made that round hill look steeper.

He knew the ocean mists that rose
    And seemed for ever staying,
When moaned the foghorn from Trevose
    And nobody was playing;

The flip of cards on winter eves,
    The whisky and the scoring,
As trees outside were stripped of leaves
    And heavy seas were roaring.

He died when early April light
    Showed red his garden sally
And under pale green spears glowed white
    His lilies of the valley:

That garden where he used to stand
    And where the robin waited
To fly and perch upon his hand
    And feed till it was sated.

The Times would never have the space
    For Ned's discreet achievements;
The public prints are not the place
    For intimate bereavements.

A gentle guest, a willing host,
Affection deeply planted—
It's strange that those we miss the most
Are those we take for granted.

Monody on the Death of a Platonist Bank Clerk

This is the lamp where he first read Whitman
    Out of the library large and free.
Every quarter the bus to Kirkstall
    Stopped and waited, but on read he.

This was his room with books in plenty:
    Dusty, now I have raised the blind—
Fenimore Cooper, Ballantyne, Henty,
    Edward Carpenter wedged behind.

These are the walls adorned with portraits,
    Camera studies and Kodak snaps;
'Camp at Pevensey'—'Scouts at Cleethorpes'—
    There he is with the lads and chaps.

This is the friend, the best and greatest,
    Pure in his surplice, smiling, true—

47

The enlarged Photomaton—that's the latest,
    Next to the coloured one ' August Blue '.

These are his pipes.   Ah! how he loved them,
    Puffed and petted them, after walks,
After tea and a frowst with crumpets,
    Puffed the smoke into serious talks.

All the lot of them, how they came to him—
    Tea and chinwag—gay young lives!
Somehow they were never the same to him
    When they married and brought their wives.

Good-bye

Some days before death
   When food's tasting sour on my tongue,
Cigarettes long abandoned,
   Disgusting now even champagne;
When I'm sweating a lot
   From the strain on a last bit of lung
And lust has gone out
   Leaving only the things of the brain;
More worthless than ever
   Will seem all the songs I have sung,
More harmless the prods of the prigs,
   Remoter the pain,
More futile the Lord Civil Servant
   As, rung upon rung,
He ascends by committees to roofs
   Far below on the plain.
But better down there in the battle
   Than here on the hill
With Judgement or nothingness waiting me,
   Lonely and chill.

Five o'Clock Shadow

This is the time of day when we in the Men's Ward
  Think "One more surge of the pain and I give up the
                                                  fight,"
When he who struggles for breath can struggle less strongly:
  This is the time of day which is worse than night.

A haze of thunder hangs on the hospital rose-beds,
  A doctors' foursome out on the links is played,
Safe in her sitting-room Sister is putting her feet up:
  This is the time of day when we feel betrayed.

Below the windows, loads of loving relations
  Rev in the car park, changing gear at the bend,
Making for home and a nice big tea and the telly:
  '' Well, we've done what we can.   It can't be long till the
                                                  end.''

This is the time of day when the weight of bedclothes
  Is harder to bear than a sharp incision of steel.
The endless anonymous croak of a cheap transistor
  Intensifies the lonely terror I feel.

50

LIGHT AND DARK

A Russell Flint

I could not speak for amazement at your beauty
   As you came down the Garrick stair,
Grey-green eyes like the turbulent Atlantic
   And floppy schoolgirl hair.

I could see you in a Sussex teashop,
   Dressed in peasant weave and brogues,
Turning over, as firelight shone on brassware,
   Last year's tea-stained *Vogues*.

I could see you as a large-eyed student,
   Frowning as you tried to learn,
Or, head flung back, the confident girl prefect,
   Thrillingly kind and stern.

I could not speak for amazement at your beauty;
   Yet, when you spoke to me,
You were calm and gentle as a rock pool
   Waiting, warm, for the sea.

Wave on wave, I plunged in them to meet you—
  In wave on wave I drown;
Calm rock pool, on the shore of my security
  Hold me when the tide goes down.

Perp. Revival i' the North

O, I wad gang tae Harrogate
    Tae a kirk by Temple Moore,
Wi' a tall choir and a lang nave
    And rush mats on the floor;
And Percy Dearmer chasubles
    And nae pews but chairs,
And there we'll sing the Sarum rite
    Tae English Hymnal airs.

It's a far cry frae Harrogate
    And mony a heathery mile
Tae a stane kirk wi' a wee spire
    And a verra wee south aisle.
The rhododendrons bloom wi'oot
    On ilka Simmer's day,
And it's there the Airl o' Feversham
    Wad hae his tenants pray;
For there's something in the painted roof
    And the mouldings round the door,
The braw bench and the plain font
    That tells o' Temple Moore.

Agricultural Caress

Keep me from Thelma's sister Pearl!
She puts my senses in a whirl,
Weakens my knees and keeps me waiting
Until my heart stops palpitating.

The debs may turn disdainful backs
On Pearl's uncouth mechanic slacks,
And outraged see the fire that lies
And smoulders in her long-lashed eyes.

Have they such weather-freckled features,
The smooth sophisticated creatures?
Ah, not to them such limbs belong,
Such animal movements sure and strong,

Such arms to take a man and press
In agricultural caress
His head to hers, and hold him there
Deep buried in her chestnut hair.

56

God shrive me from this morning lust
For supple farm girls: if you must,
Send the cold daughter of an earl—
But spare me Thelma's sister Pearl!

Narcissus

Yes, it was Bedford Park the vision came from—
    de Morgan lustre glowing round the hearth,
And that sweet flower which self-love takes its name from
    Nodding among the lilies in the garth,
And Arnold Dolmetsch touching the spinet,
And Mother, Chiswick's earliest suffragette.

I was a delicate boy—my parents' only—
    And highly strung.   My father was in trade.
And how I loved, when Mother left me lonely,
    To watch old Martha spice the marmalade,
Or help with flower arrangements in the lobby
Before I went to find my playmate Bobby.

We'ld go for walks, we bosom boyfriends would
    (For Bobby's watching sisters drove us mad),
And when we just did nothing we were good,
    But when we touched each other we were bad.
I found this out when Mother said one day
She thought we were unwholesome in our play.

So Bobby and I were parted. Bobby dear,

 I didn't want my tea.   I heard your sisters
Playing at hide-and-seek with you quite near

 As off the garden gate I picked the blisters.
Oh tell me, Mother, what I mustn't do—
Then, Bobby, I can play again with you.

For I know hide-and-seek's most secret places

 More than your sisters do.   And you and I
Can scramble into them and leave no traces,

 Nothing above us but the twigs and sky,
Nothing below us but the leaf-mould chilly
Where we can warm and hug each other silly.

My Mother wouldn't tell me why she hated

 The things we did, and why they pained her so.
She said a fate far worse than death awaited

 People who did the things we didn't know,
And then she said I was her precious child,
And once there was a man called Oscar Wilde.

" Open your story book and find a tale

 Of ladyes fayre and deeds of derring-do,
Or good Sir Gawaine and the Holy Grail,

59

Mother will read her boy a page or two
Before she goes, this Woman's Suffrage Week,
To hear that clever Mrs Pankhurst speak.

Sleep with your hands above your head. That's right—
    And let no evil thoughts pollute the dark.''
She rose, and lowered the incandescent light.
    I heard her footsteps die down Bedford Park.
Mother where are you?   Bobby, Bobby, where?
I clung for safety to my teddy bear.

The Cockney Amorist

Oh when my love, my darling,
   You've left me here alone,
I'll walk the streets of London
   Which once seemed all our own.

The vast suburban churches
   Together we have found:
The ones which smelt of gaslight
   The ones in incense drown'd;
I'll use them now for praying in
   And not for looking round.

No more the Hackney Empire
   Shall find us in its stalls
When on the limelit crooner
   The thankful curtain falls,
And soft electric lamplight
   Reveals the gilded walls.

I will not go to Finsbury Park
　　The putting course to see
Nor cross the crowded High Road
　　To Williamsons' to tea,
For these and all the other things
　　Were part of you and me.

I love you, oh my darling,
　　And what I can't make out
Is why since you have left me
　　I'm somehow still about.

Harvest Hymn

We spray the fields and scatter
    The poison on the ground
So that no wicked wild flowers
    Upon our farm be found.
We like whatever helps us
    To line our purse with pence;
The twenty-four-hour broiler-house
    And neat electric fence.

    All concrete sheds around us
    And Jaguars in the yard,
    The telly lounge and deep-freeze
    Are ours from working hard.

We fire the fields for harvest,
    The hedges swell the flame,
The oak trees and the cottages
    From which our fathers came.
We give no compensation,

The earth is ours today,
And if we lose on arable,
Then bungalows will pay.

All concrete sheds . . . etc.

Meditation on the A30

A man on his own in a car
   Is revenging himself on his wife;
He opens the throttle and bubbles with dottle
   And puffs at his pitiful life.

" She's losing her looks very fast,
   She loses her temper all day;
That lorry won't let me get past,
   This Mini is blocking my way.

" Why can't you step on it and shift her!
   I can't go on crawling like this!
At breakfast she said that she wished I was dead—
   Thank heavens we don't have to kiss.

" I'd like a nice blonde on my knee
   And one who won't argue or nag.
Who dares to come hooting at *me*?
   I only give way to a Jag.

" You're barmy or plastered, I'll pass you, you bastard—
   I *will* overtake you.   I *will*! "
As he clenches his pipe, his moment is ripe
   And the corner's accepting its kill.

Inexpensive Progress

Encase your legs in nylons,
Bestride your hills with pylons
   O age without a soul;
Away with gentle willows
And all the elmy billows
   That through your valleys roll.

Let's say good-bye to hedges
And roads with grassy edges
   And winding country lanes;
Let all things travel faster
Where motor-car is master
   Till only Speed remains.

Destroy the ancient inn-signs
But strew the roads with tin signs
   'Keep Left,' 'M4,' 'Keep Out!'
Command, instruction, warning,
Repetitive adorning
   The rockeried roundabout;

For every raw obscenity
Must have its small ' amenity,'
    Its patch of shaven green,
And hoardings look a wonder
In banks of floribunda
    With floodlights in between.

Leave no old village standing
Which could provide a landing
    For aeroplanes to roar,
But spare such cheap defacements
As huts with shattered casements
    Unlived-in since the war.

Let no provincial High Street
Which might be your or my street
    Look as it used to do,
But let the chain stores place here
Their miles of black glass facia
    And traffic thunder through.

And if there is some scenery,
Some unpretentious greenery,
    Surviving anywhere,

68

It does not need protecting
For soon we'll be erecting
   A Power Station there.

When all our roads are lighted
By concrete monsters sited
   Like gallows overhead,
Bathed in the yellow vomit
Each monster belches from it,
   We'll know that we are dead.

Mortality

The first-class brains of a senior civil servant
   Shiver and shatter and fall
As the steering column of his comfortable Humber
   Batters in the bony wall.
All those delicate little re-adjustments
   '' On the one hand, if we proceed
With the *ad hoc* policy hitherto adapted
   To individual need . . .
On the other hand, too rigid an arrangement
   Might, of itself, perforce . . .
I would like to submit for the Minister's concurrence
   The following alternative course,
Subject to revision and reconsideration
   In the light our experience gains . . .''
And this had to happen at the corner where the by-pass
   Comes into Egham out of Staines.
That very near miss for an All Souls' Fellowship
   The recent compensation of a 'K'—
The first-class brains of a senior civil servant
   Are sweetbread on the road today.

PERSONAL

Reproof Deserved
or
After the Lecture

When I saw the grapefruit drying, cherry in each centre
lying

And a dozen guests expected at the table's polished oak,

Then I knew, my lecture finished, I'ld be feeling quite
diminished

Talking on, but unprotected, so that all my spirit broke.

" Have you read the last Charles Morgan? " " Are you
writing for the organ

Which is published as a vital adjunct to our cultural
groups? ''

'' This year some of us are learning all *The Lady's Not for
Burning*

For a poetry recital we are giving to the troops.''

'' Mr Betjeman, I grovel before critics of the novel,

Tell me, if I don't offend you, have you written one your-
self?

You haven't? Then the one I wrote is (not that I expect a
notice)

Something I would like to send you, just for keeping on
your shelf.''

" Betjeman, I bet your racket brings you in a pretty packet

Raising the old lecture curtain, writing titbits here and there.

But, by Jove, your hair is thinner, since you came to us in Pinner,

And you're fatter now, I'm certain. What you need is country air."

This and that way conversation, till I turn in desperation

To a kind face (can I doubt it?) mercifully mute so far.

" Oh," it says, " I missed the lecture, wasn't it on architecture?

Do please tell me all about it, what you do and who you are."

Caprice

I sat only two tables off from the one I was sacked at,
> Just three years ago,
And here was another meringue like the one which I hacked
>> at
> When pride was brought low
And the coffee arrived—the place which she had to use tact
>> at
> For striking the blow.

" I'm making some changes next week in the organisation
> And though I admire
Your work for me, John, yet the need to increase circulation
> Means you must retire:
An outlook more global than yours is the qualification
> I really require.''

Oh sickness of sudden betrayal!   Oh purblind Creator!
> Oh friendship denied!
I stood on the pavement and wondered which loss was the
>> greater—

The cash or the pride.

Explanations to make to subordinates, bills to pay later

Churned up my inside.

Cricket Master
(AN INCIDENT)

My undergraduate eyes beholding,
    As I climbed your slope, Cat Hill:
Emerald chestnut fans unfolding,
    Symbols of my hope, Cat Hill,
What cared I for past disaster,
Applicant for cricket master,
Nothing much of cricket knowing,
Conscious but of money owing?
    Somehow I would cope, Cat Hill.

'' The sort of man we want must be prepared
To take our first eleven.   Many boys
From last year's team are with us.   You will find
Their bowling's pretty good and they are keen.''
'' And so am I, Sir, very keen indeed.''
Oh where's mid-on?   And what is silly point?
Do six balls make an over?   Help me, God!
'' Of course you'll get some first-class cricket too;

The MCC send down an A team here.''
My bluff had worked.   I sought the common-room,
Of last term's pipe-smoke faintly redolent.
It waited empty with its worn arm-chairs
For senior bums to mine, when in there came
A fierce old eagle in whose piercing eye
I saw that instant-registered dislike
Of all unhealthy aesthetes such as me.
'' I'm Winters—you're our other new recruit
And here's another new man—Barnstaple.''
He introduced a thick Devonian.
'' Let's go and have some practice in the nets.
You'd better go in first.''   With but one pad,
No gloves, and knees that knocked in utter fright,
Vainly I tried to fend the hail of balls
Hurled at my head by brutal Barnstaple
And at my shins by Winters.   Nasty quiet
Followed my poor performance.   When the sun
Had sunk behind the fringe of Hadley Wood
And Barnstaple and I were left alone
Among the ash-trays of the common-room,
He murmured in his soft West-country tones:
'' D'you know what Winters told me, Betjeman?
He didn't think you'd ever held a bat.''

The trusting boys returned.   " We're jolly glad
You're on our side, Sir, in the trial match."
" But I'm no good at all." " Oh yes, you are."
When I was out first ball, they said " Bad luck!
You hadn't got your eye in."   Still I see
Barnstaple's smile of undisguised contempt,
Still feel the sting of Winters' silent sneer.
Disgraced, demoted to the seventh game,
Even the boys had lost their faith in me.
God guards his aesthetes.   If by chance these lines
Are read by one who in some common-room
Has had his bluff called, let him now take heart:
In every school there is a sacred place
More holy than the chapel.   Ours was yours:
I mean, of course, the first-eleven pitch.
Here in the welcome break from morning work,
The heavier boys, of milk and biscuits full,
Sat on the roller while we others pushed
Its weighty cargo slowly up and down.
We searched the grass for weeds, caressed the turf,
Lay on our stomachs squinting down its length
To see that all was absolutely smooth.

The prize-day neared.   And, on the eve before.
We masters hung our college blazers out

In readiness for tomorrow.   Matron made
A final survey of the boys' best clothes—
Clean shirts.   Clean collars. '' Rice, your jacket's torn.
Bring it to me this instant!''   Supper done,
Barnstaple drove his round-nosed Morris out
And he and I and Vera Spencer-Clarke,
Our strong gymnasium mistress, squashed ourselves
Into the front and rattled to The Cock.

Sweet bean-fields then were scenting Middlesex;
Narrow lanes led between the dairy-farms
To ponds reflecting weather-boarded inns.
There on the wooden bench outside The Cock
Sat Barnstaple, Miss Spencer-Clarke and I,
At last forgetful of tomorrow's dread
And gazing into sky-blue Hertfordshire.
Three pints for Barnstaple, three halves for me,
Sherry of course for Vera Spencer-Clarke.

Pre-prize-day nerves?   Or too much bitter beer?
What had that evening done to Barnstaple?
I only know that singing we returned;
The more we sang, the faster Barnstaple
Drove his old Morris, swerving down the drive
And in and out the rhododendron clumps,
Over the very playing-field itself,

And then—oh horror!—right across the pitch
Not once, but twice or thrice. The mark of tyres
Next day was noticed at the Parents' Match.
That settled Barnstaple and he was sacked,
While I survived him, lasting three more terms.

Shops and villas have invaded
    Your chestnut quiet there, Cat Hill.
Cricket field and pitch degraded,
    Nothing did they spare, Cat Hill.
Vera Spencer-Clarke is married
And the rest are dead and buried;
I am thirty summers older,
Richer, wickeder and colder,
    Fuller too of care, Cat Hill.